Female genital mutilation

A Joint WHO/UNICEF/UNFPA Statement

WORLD HEALTH ORGANIZATION
GENEVA
1997

WHO Library Cataloguing in Publication Data

Female genital mutilation : a joint WHO/UNICEF/UNFPA
    statement.

    1. Circumcision, Female   2. International cooperation

    ISBN 92 4 156186 6 (NLM Classification: WP 660)

The World Health Organization welcomes requests for permission to reproduce or translate its publications, in part or in full. Applications and enquiries should be addressed to the Office of Publications, World Health Organization, Geneva, Switzerland, which will be glad to provide the latest information on any changes made to the text, plans for new editions, and reprints and translations already available.

Typeset in Hong Kong

Printed in Switzerland

97/11223-Best-set/Triada-13000

Contents

Page

Introduction   1

What is female genital mutilation?   3

Health complications   7

International agreements   10

National and community action   13

International approaches and actions   16

Conclusion   20

Introduction

All societies have norms of care and behaviour based on age, life stage, gender and social class. These norms, often referred to as traditional practices, may be beneficial or harmless, but some may be harmful. Those traditional practices relating to female children, relations between women and men, and marriage and sexuality often have a harmful effect on women and girls. There are many examples of this. Son preference or the high value placed on sons may lead to discrimination against girls with serious health consequences for them. In extreme cases it may lead to prenatal sex selection or the infanticide of female infants. Traditional payments made by a husband to obtain a wife serve to strengthen the attitude that women are property and can lead to physical abuse, intimidation, or even death. Marriage and childbearing before girls have reached physical and psychosocial maturity also create many health risks for young women.

One deeply rooted traditional practice that has severe health consequences for girls and women is female genital mutilation, sometimes referred to as female circumcision. Female genital mutilation reinforces the inequity suffered by girls and women in the communities where it is practised and must be addressed if their health, social and economic development needs are to be met. The arguments against female genital mutilation are based on universally recognized human rights, including the rights to integrity of the person and the highest attainable level of physical and mental health. The health consequences of the practice vary according to the procedure used. Nevertheless, female genital mutilation is universally unacceptable because it is an infringement on the physical and psychosexual integrity of women and girls and is a form of violence against them.

In presenting this statement, the purpose is neither to criticize nor to condemn. Even though cultural practices may appear senseless or destructive from the standpoint of others, they have meaning and fulfil a function for those who practise them. However, culture is not static; it is in constant flux, adapting and reforming. People will change their behaviour when they understand the hazards and indignity of harmful practices and when they realize that it is possible to give up harmful practices without giving up meaningful aspects of their culture. The role of the World Health Organization (WHO), the United Nations Children's Fund (UNICEF) and the United Nations Population Fund (UNFPA) is to support global, national and community efforts for the elimination of female genital mutilation in order to achieve health and well-being for women, girls, their families and communities.

What is female genital mutilation?

Definition

Female genital mutilation comprises all procedures involving partial or total removal of the external female genitalia or other injury to the female genital organs whether for cultural or other non-therapeutic reasons.

Classification

The different types of female genital mutilation known to be practised are as follows:

Type I   Excision of the prepuce, with or without excision of part or all of the clitoris.

Type II   Excision of the clitoris with partial or total excision of the labia minora.

Type III Excision of part or all of the external genitalia and stitching/narrowing of the vaginal opening (infibulation).

Type IV   Unclassified: includes pricking, piercing or incising of the clitoris and/or labia; stretching of the clitoris and/or labia; cauterization by burning of the clitoris and surrounding tissue; scraping of tissue surrounding the vaginal orifice (angurya cuts) or cutting of the vagina (gishiri cuts); introduction of corrosive substances or herbs into the vagina to cause bleeding or for the purposes of tightening or narrowing it; and any other procedure that falls under the definition of female genital mutilation given above.

The procedures described above are irreversible and their effects last a lifetime.

Practitioners

In cultures where it is an accepted norm, female genital mutilation is usually performed by a traditional practitioner with crude instruments and without anaesthetic. Among the more affluent sectors of society it may be performed in a health care facility by qualified health personnel.

Age and reasons for female genital mutilation

The age at which female genital mutilation is carried out varies from area to area. Reports indicate that it is performed on infants a few days old, on children between 6 and 10 years of age, in adolescence and occasionally in adulthood. The reasons for the practice have been reported in a number of research papers, interviews and statements. These reasons fall into five groups:

- *psychosexual reasons* — reduction or elimination of the sensitive tissue of the outer genitalia, particularly the clitoris, in order to attenuate sexual desire in the female, maintain chastity and virginity before marriage and fidelity during marriage, and increase male sexual pleasure;
- *sociological reasons* — identification with the cultural heritage, initiation of girls into womanhood, social integration and the maintenance of social cohesion;
- *hygiene and aesthetic reasons* — the external female genitalia are considered dirty and unsightly and should be removed to promote hygiene and provide aesthetic appeal;
- *myths* — enhancement of fertility and promotion of child survival;
- *religious reasons* — female genital mutilation is practised by Muslims, Christians (Catholics, Protestants, Copts), animists and nonbelievers in a range of communities. It has, however, frequently been carried out by some Muslim communities in the genuine belief that it is demanded by the Islamic faith. However, the practice of female genital mutilation predates Islam and there is no substantive evidence that it is a religious requirement of Islam.

Prevalence and distribution

Most of the girls and women who have undergone genital mutilation live in 28 African countries, although some live in Asia. They are also increasingly found in Europe, Australia, Canada and the USA, primarily among immigrants from Africa and southwestern Asia. It is estimated that over 130 million girls and women in Africa have undergone some form of female genital mutilation. The map (overleaf) shows the areas of the world in which female genital mutilation has been reported to occur.

The commonest type of female genital mutilation is excision of the clitoris and the labia minora, accounting for up to 80% of all cases. The most extreme form is infibulation, which constitutes about 15% of all procedures. The incidence of infibulation is much higher in Djibouti, Somalia and northern Sudan, with a consequent higher rate of complications. Infibulation is also reported in southern Egypt, Eritrea, Ethiopia, northern Kenya, Mali and Nigeria. At current rates of population increase, and with slow decline in these procedures, it is estimated that at least 2 million girls are at risk of genital mutilation every year.

Areas of the world in which female genital mutilation has been reported to occur

WHO 96341

■ Areas in which female genital
mutilation has been reported

● Female genital mutilation practised
among some immigrant communities

The designations employed and the presentation of material on this map do not imply the expression of any opinion whatsoever on the part of the World Health Organization concerning
the legal status of any country, territory, city or area or of its authorities, or concerning the delimitation of its frontiers or boundaries.
Information on the map is based mainly on partial and incomplete data.

Health complications

The immediate and long-term health consequences of female genital mutilation vary according to the type and severity of the procedure performed.

Immediate complications

The immediate complications include severe pain, shock, haemorrhage, tetanus or sepsis, urine retention, ulceration of the genital region and injury to adjacent tissue. Haemorrhage and infection can be of such a magnitude as to cause death. More recently, concern has arisen about possible transmission of the human immunodeficiency virus (HIV) due to the use of one instrument in multiple operations, but this has not been the subject of detailed research. In some cases where infibulation prevents or impedes vaginal intercourse, anal intercourse may be used as an alternative. The resulting damage to tissue is also a possible route of infection by HIV.

Long-term complications

Reported long-term consequences include cysts and abscesses, keloid scar formation, damage to the urethra resulting in urinary incontinence, dyspareunia (painful sexual intercourse) and sexual dysfunction. Infibulation can cause severe scar formation, difficulty in urinating and during menstruation, recurrent bladder and urinary tract infection and infertility. Because infibulation often makes intercourse difficult, it is sometimes necessary to cut open the bridge of skin created by the labia majora. Cutting may also be necessary when giving birth. Although few reliable data exist, it is likely that the risk of maternal death and stillbirth is greatly increased, particularly in the absence of skilled health personnel and appropriate facilities. During childbirth, the risk of haemorrhage and infection is greatly increased. Female genital mutilation may also be associated with long-term maternal morbidity (e.g. vesicovaginal fistula).

Psychosexual and psychological health

Almost all types of female genital mutilation involve the removal of part or all of the clitoris, which is the main female sexual organ, equivalent in its anatomy and physiology to the male penis. The more severe types, such as infibulation, remove larger parts of the genitals and close off the vagina, leaving areas of tough scar tissue in place of the sensitive genitalia, thus creating permanent damage and dysfunction. Sexual dysfunction in both partners may result from painful intercourse and reduced sexual sensitivity following clitoridectomy and narrowing of the vaginal opening.

Genital mutilation may leave a lasting mark on the life and mind of the woman who has undergone it. The psychological complications may be submerged deep in the child's subconscious and may trigger behavioural disturbances. The loss of trust and confidence in care-givers has been reported as a possible serious effect. In the longer term, women may suffer feelings of incompleteness, anxiety, depression, chronic irritability and frigidity. They may experience marital conflicts. Many girls and women, traumatized by their experience but with no acceptable means of expressing their fears, suffer in silence.

The medicalization of female genital mutilation

WHO has consistently and unequivocally advised that female genital mutilation in any form should not be practised by health professionals in any setting — including hospitals or other health establishments. WHO's position rests on the basic ethics of health care whereby unnecessary bodily mutilation cannot be condoned by health providers. Genital mutilation is harmful to girls and women and medicalization of the procedure does not eliminate this harm. Medicalization is also inappropriate as it reinforces the continuation of the practice by seeming to legitimize it. In communities where infibulation is the norm, it has been noted that many families revert to clitoridectomy when health education programmes commence. However, the formal policy messages must consistently convey that all forms of female genital mutilation must be stopped.

International agreements

International human rights covenants underscore the obligations of United Nations Member States to respect and to ensure the protection and promotion of human rights, including the rights to non-discrimination, to integrity of the person and to the highest attainable standard of physical and mental health. In this regard, most governments in countries where female genital mutilation is practised have ratified several United Nations Conventions and Declarations that make provision for the promotion and protection of the health of girls and women, including the elimination of female genital mutilation, as indicated in the box.

1948   The Universal Declaration of Human Rights proclaimed the right of all human beings to live in conditions that enable them to enjoy good health and health care.

1966   The International Covenants on Civil and Political Rights and on Economic, Social and Cultural Rights condemned discrimination on the grounds of sex, and recognized the universal right to the highest attainable standard of physical and mental health.

1979   The Convention on the Elimination of All Forms of Discrimination against Women can be interpreted to require States Parties to take action against female genital mutilation, namely:

- "to take all appropriate measures, including legislation, to modify or abolish existing laws, regulations, customs and practices which constitute discrimination against women" (Art. 2.f);

- "to modify the social and cultural patterns of conduct of men and women, with a view to achieving the elimination of prejudices and customary and all other practices which are based on the idea of the inferiority or the superiority of either of the sexes or on stereotyped roles for men and women" (Art. 5.a);

1990   The Convention on the Rights of the Child protects the right to equality irrespective of sex (Art. 2), to freedom from all forms of mental and physical violence and maltreatment (Art. 19.1), to the highest attainable standard of health (Art. 24.1), and to freedom from torture or cruel, inhuman or degrading treatment (Art. 37.a). Article 24.3 of the Convention explicitly requires States to take all effective and appropriate measures to abolish traditional practices prejudicial to the health of children.

1993   The Vienna Declaration and the Programme of Action of the World Conference on Human Rights expanded the international human rights agenda to include gender-based violations which include female genital mutilation.

1993   The Declaration on Violence Against Women expressly states in its article 2:

"Violence against women shall be understood to encompass, but not be limited to, the following:

(a) Physical, sexual and psychological violence occurring in the family, including . . . dowry-related violence . . . female genital mutilation and other traditional practices harmful to women . . ."

1994   The Programme of Action of the International Conference on Population and Development (ICPD) included recommendations on female genital mutilation which commit governments and communities to:

"urgently take steps to stop the practice of female genital mutilation and to protect women and girls from all such similar unnecessary and dangerous practices".

1995   The Platform for Action of the Fourth World Conference on Women included a section on the girl child and urged governments, international organizations and nongovernmental groups to develop policies and programmes to eliminate all forms of discrimination against the girl child, including female genital mutilation.

In order to make these agreements meaningful, mechanisms must be developed to implement them at grassroots level and concerted efforts must be made to protect the rights of girls and women.

National and community action

In the last decade, many organizations and individuals have attempted community-based activities aimed at the elimination of female genital mutilation. Much experience has been gained in bringing the problem to the attention of political, religious and community leaders and in creating an atmosphere of political support for the elimination of the practice. There is increasing recognition that the cultural purpose of female genital mutilation varies as widely as the type of procedure performed and that a full understanding of women's position and of gender relations within the particular sociocultural and economic context is required in order to eliminate the practice. Efforts to stop it must therefore not be limited to the medical model of disease eradication but must be part of a multidisciplinary approach. While there is not a great body of successful experience, those involved in action against female genital mutilation concur in the overall approaches to be taken, as follows:

■ adoption of clear national policies for the abolition of female genital mutilation including, where appropriate, the enactment of legislation to prohibit it;

■ establishment of interagency teams that bring together representatives of relevant government ministries, nongovernmental organizations and professional organizations and associations to ensure action to eliminate female genital mutilation;

■ support for research into all aspects of female genital mutilation, including incidence, prevalence, the main reasons why it continues to be practised, and health consequences, as well as operations research on interventions for eliminating it;

■ organization of strong community outreach and family life education programmes that involve village and religious leaders and address the main reasons for continuing the practice (experience shows that, where leadership is enlightened and committed, information and education activities are more successful);

- emphasis on sustainability in health and development programmes; and integration of action to eliminate female genital mutilation into existing health education, child protection and community development efforts;
- use of consistent messages and all available channels to communicate information to all sectors of the public (mass media, popular music, drama and crafts, group discussion sessions, as well as one-to-one counselling, have been successfully used to target women and men, old and young, community elders and family members);
- prohibition of the medicalization of female genital mutilation, and provision of professional guidance and training for health professionals on the elimination of the practice and on the management of its health consequences;
- ensuring that there is appropriate rehabilitation and treatment for women and girls who suffer problems related to genital mutilation (including counselling so that women and adolescent girls have the opportunity to express their fears and concerns about their health and sexuality);
- support for and encouragement of nongovernmental organizations, particularly women's groups and education and advocacy groups (such groups are important catalysts for starting open discussion of female genital mutilation where such discussion was formerly considered taboo);
- targeting of information at traditional healers and birth attendants who practise female genital mutilation, and provision of training to prevent efforts for the elimination of the practice being undermined by indifference or opposition;
- avoidance of intervention strategies which lead to the creation of a cultural vacuum (where appropriate, alternative rites of passage involving gift-giving and celebration should be encouraged for young girls to help promote positive female traditional values without causing physical and psychological damage);
- targeting of young couples with materials that give high esteem to girls and women who have not undergone genital mutilation, and provision of support to parents to enable them to resist pressures to expose their daughters to the practice (young people are often in the vanguard of creating

new social norms, but at the same time there is a need for sensitivity when working with young women who have already undergone genital mutilation);

■ enlistment of men's participation so that as women's attitudes begin to change they find support among brothers, fathers, friends and partners.

Since national bodies and community groups may be at different stages in the drive to eliminate female genital mutilation, the most appropriate and effective combination of the above approaches should be used according to the particular situation.

Strategic considerations

It must be recognized that women are frequently preoccupied with ensuring their own and their families' survival and may not see female genital mutilation as an immediate priority. The elimination of female genital mutilation is also a step towards the achievement of gender equity, equality and women's empowerment. Seeing it as part of a broader effort to improve women's status and health, including their sexual and reproductive health, may give it wider appeal. Efforts towards elimination of the practice should also be included in programmes for adolescent and child health, family planning and safe motherhood. In the long term, the education of girls and women will enable attitudes to be changed and traditions transformed.

Legislation against female genital mutilation is important both because it represents a formal expression of public disapproval and because it is the means by which governments can establish official sanctions. However, the kind of legal sanction and the point at which it is introduced are critical concerns. If most people in a society value female genital mutilation highly and consider it a necessary practice, then legislation in the absence of community-based action is an insufficient and inappropriate strategy. Legislation against female genital mutilation is most effective when a system of child monitoring and protection is in operation, when there is widespread education of communities and mobilization of public opinion against the practice, and when women and communities are involved in efforts to abolish the practice.

International approaches and actions

The United Nations is committed to the protection of human rights and has emphasized the need to advance and protect the lives and health, including the psychological and sexual health, of women and children. It is therefore the duty of WHO, UNICEF and UNFPA to support policies and programmes that bring an end to the damaging practice of female genital mutilation in all its forms, and prevent it becoming institutionalized within the formal health system.

In order to coordinate activities for the prevention of female genital mutilation and to ensure that the issue is seen in the broader context of women's reproductive health and rights, various approaches will need to be developed. These include:

- raising the awareness of United Nations agencies, funding and development assistance agencies, policy-makers, health authorities and influential leaders in health and other sectors, about the effects of female genital mutilation on health and on social and economic development, and providing technical assistance to these bodies;
- promoting, providing technical support to, and mobilizing resources for national and local groups that will initiate community-based activities aimed at eliminating female genital mutilation and other harmful practices that affect the health of women and children;
- assisting national authorities, nongovernmental organizations and other interested groups in the development of policies which reflect the legal and human rights aspects of female genital mutilation; defining programme priorities and research needs;
- developing prototype materials (for adaptation to local needs) that convey essential messages on the implications of female genital mutilation for health, the protection of children, and

human rights, targeted at policy-makers and decision-makers, at various levels of the health care system (formal and traditional) and at other sectors;

■ developing guidelines for training health care professionals in the prevention of female genital mutilation and in the care of women subjected to the practice, particularly with respect to pregnancy, delivery and psychosexual health;

■ assisting national authorities to review and revise school curricula to ensure that girls and women are portrayed in a balanced and non-stereotypical way.

Proposed action by WHO, UNICEF and UNFPA

Reasons for the slow progress in eliminating female genital mutilation include the lack of coordination of prevention programmes and limited investment of resources in them. A well designed and well coordinated campaign against the practice, with appropriate technical expertise and adequate levels of funding, should bring about a major decline in female genital mutilation in 10 years and lead to its elimination within three generations.

Since female genital mutilation concerns both the health and rights of women and children, it is a good model for interagency collaboration. WHO, UNICEF, UNFPA and the other United Nations agencies each have their special strengths and focus, and their activities complement each other. This can be seen in the agencies' proposed actions on female genital mutilation, as described below.

WHO

There is considerable knowledge about the epidemiology and consequences of female genital mutilation, but there are still major gaps in understanding the extent of the problem, its health impact and the kinds of interventions that can be successful in eliminating it. Part of WHO's future activities for the elimination of female genital mutilation will be focused on increasing knowledge through a research and development programme and promoting technically sound policies and approaches. This will include ensuring that female genital mutilation is seen as an issue that relates to women's health, reproductive health and human rights.

WHO has special responsibility in the development of training materials, including the preparation of guidelines to equip health care workers with the appropriate knowledge, skills and attitudes for preventing and eliminating female genital mutilation and for managing the health complications that result from the practice. WHO will use its official links with professional organizations of health workers to build on existing training activities and develop educational materials for professionals. WHO will also strengthen its partnership with governments, nongovernmental organizations, scientists, reproductive health programme managers and policy-makers, human rights advocates, and the United Nations agencies, with the common goal of eliminating female genital mutilation.

UNICEF

Most of UNICEF's efforts for the elimination of female genital mutilation take place through its field offices and country programmes. These efforts involve a range of approaches, particularly the provision of support to community-based organizations engaged in information, education, communication and training relating to the prevention of female genital mutilation. While many UNICEF country offices support activities targeted at eliminating the practice, these activities are often integrated into broader programmes in the areas of health, education, communication and the improvement of women's status. Particular emphasis is placed on working with youth organizations and women's groups to make their members aware of the dangers of female genital mutilation and to sensitize them to the need to end the practice.

UNFPA

UNFPA will continue to advocate the elimination of female genital mutilation wherever it occurs, and will support the review and revision of national policies, laws, regulations and traditional practices pertaining to reproductive health which serve to perpetuate it. In addition, UNFPA supports the information, education and communication efforts of national organizations — governmental, nongovernmental and private — against female genital mutilation, supports sociocultural research to identify the factors that underly the persistence of the practice, and supports the collection of data on its incidence and prevalence.

Conclusion

This joint statement of WHO, UNICEF and UNFPA expresses the common purpose of the three organizations in supporting the efforts of governments and communities to promote and protect the health and development of women and children. Female genital mutilation is not only a dangerous practice, but it is an important issue for our attention in view of the Goals and Plan of Action of the World Summit for Children, the Programme of Action of the International Conference on Population and Development, the Plan of Action of the United Nations Fourth World Conference on Women, the Convention on the Elimination of All Forms of Discrimination against Women, the Convention on the Rights of the Child, and several World Health Assembly and WHO Regional Committee resolutions.

In order to deal with female genital mutilation effectively, it is necessary to promote awareness of the problem by educating the public, health workers and those who carry out the practice on all its health and psychosocial consequences. This calls for the active involvement of political leaders, professionals, development workers, local communities and their leaders, and women's groups and organizations. International advocacy and collaboration have a role to play in complementing the efforts of local groups with due sensitivity and care.